Wait for your Turn

VIRTUE STORIES

Lalita Iyer

Om KIDZ
An imprint of Om Books International

Mimi's most favourite place in the world was the good, old library in the centre of the town. Her mother took her there every weekend. She loved to spend hours crossing the ancient corridors, browsing through piles of books. Even the book lending system was old-style! She could browse and read as much as she liked, but she could only take four books home. For Mimi, this was always a difficult decision.

Mimi was lost in the wonders of ancient Egypt in a book of illustrated pictures, when her mother tapped her on the shoulder. It was time to go home.

Mimi did an eeny-meeny-mynah-moh and picked up four books from the pile she had kept aside to borrow. Just when she was about to reach the counter, a little boy, who seemed to be in a great hurry, ran past her and got there before she did.

RHYMES

The kind lady behind the counter, Mrs Richards, saw Mimi coming towards her first and requested the boy to wait. But since he was in a hurry to pull his books out, he didn't even see her hand gesture and as he pulled Cursed Child out, his pencil case spilled out too, as he had forgotten to zip it. Everything fell on the floor – including his origami birds, some paper balls, lots of coins, his football erasers and god knows what else!

RHYMES

By this time, three other children were in the queue and Mimi was the first. The boy got up, picked his things and looked at her apologetically. She smiled. 'It's okay, you may go first,' she said. Mrs Richards entered the book codes and stamped them with the due date for return. She then handed the books back to the boy. He hurriedly tried stuffing them all into his small bag. They kept spilling out and he was getting more and more delayed.

Mimi waited patiently for him to leave. She, then, cheerfully went up to the counter and handed her books to Mrs Richards. The strict lady looked through her glasses, took her books, punched the numbers in and asked Mimi if she would like to come in to her side of the counter.

Mimi was pleasantly surprised and excited at this. She couldn't believe her luck!

The little boy stopped what he was doing, stood up, and with his mouth open, saw what Mimi was going to be doing. If only I had waited my turn, I too might have got to do this, he thought.

Once Mrs Richards let Mimi in through her little side gate to her side of the counter, she handed Mimi the date stamp. She then got her to check today's date, helped her add 10 days to it and asked her to turn the stamp rails one by one and punch it on the books.

Mimi was grinning from ear to ear and was clearly having a lot of fun and feeling all important.

Once done, Mimi picked up her books and thanked Mrs Richards for having let her do the stamping. Mrs Richards in return, thanked Mimi and welcomed her to come again.

As she walked away with her mother, Mimi shared her wonder. ’Mom, who would have thought I would be able to live my dream of being a librarian today, just like the stylish Mrs Richards!’ Her mother looked at her lovingly and hugged her. ‘Mimi, this was the reward you got for being polite and kind in waiting patiently for your turn!’